# Seesaw Marjorie Daw

Seesaw Marjorie Daw,

Johnnie shall have a new master.

He shall have but a penny a day,

Because he can't work any faster.

# Activity 1

## The Park

Do you have a park nearby?
Do you have a favourite park toy?

Work in teams to design and make a park picture.
Make sure you show all the park toys on which children play.
Make sure others will know what the toys are.

**You will need**

paints    sticky paper    paper
crayons

First, think about what you are trying to do.
Talk about what is needed in your team.
Think about how you will do it.
Make sure everybody has a job to do. Make a plan.

Get ready. Steady. Go!

How does it look?
Tell everyone about the park.

at the park

# The Seesaw

Do you like playing on the seesaw?
Can you remember how it works?
Try to draw a picture showing how the seesaw works.

Make a seesaw.

**You will need**

a plank of wood

a roller

Can you choose some children who you can balance on the seesaw?
Try it out.
How did you choose the children?

You can use the seesaw to sort out a group of children from heaviest to lightest.
Make a class chart.

Play seesaws with someone who is much lighter than you.
How can you balance the seesaw?

## Learning about levers

The seesaw is a machine called a lever.

Here are the special names for the parts of a lever.

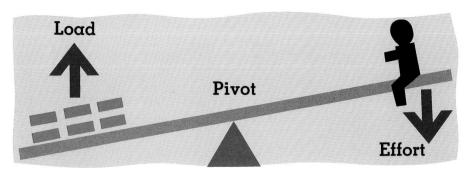

★ Find the pivot on your seesaw.

★ Find the place for the load.

★ Do you need a lot or a little effort to move your load?

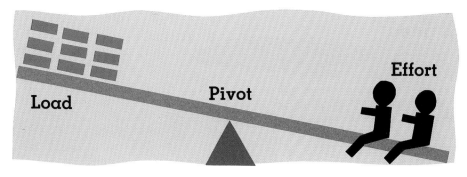

Make a big class seesaw picture which shows all the parts of the lever. Label them with the special names.

4

# The law of levers

## You will need

a metre rule · some weights · a roller

Find the law of levers.
Can you make 100 grams
balance 100 grams?

Measure the distance of the
load from the pivot.
Measure the distance of the
effort from the pivot.
Draw a picture of it all and
put in your measurements.

Can you now make 50 grams balance 100 grams?
Tell everyone how you did it.
Measure the two distances again.

Draw another picture and put in your new measurements.

The pivot isn't always in the middle.
Play with your lever. Can you invent new uses for it?

# Activity 5

## The force of levers

There are lever inventions all around you.

Try these lever problems.

★ Find the easiest way to remove a tin lid with a spoon handle.

★ Find the easiest way of lifting a rock from the ground with a spade.

Can you find the effort, the load and the pivot in each problem?

Can you find new ways to use levers?
Draw some of your best ideas

# Design and make a mobile

### You will need
Your choice of materials from the junk box.

First of all, think about the problem of balancing the mobile. Try out a few ideas. Do they work?

Now think about your decorations.
Try out a few ideas.

Make a plan of what you are going to do.
Get everything ready.

Make it as neatly as you can and hang it up.
Tell everyone about how you solved your problems.
Have you found out any new laws?

# Activity 7

## Design and make a fearsome monster!

Look at a pair of scissors.
Can you see they are levers?
Look at lots of scissors.

★ How are they the same?
★ How are they different?
★ Which levers work best?

Now we will make a machine with the scissor action.
Then we will change it into a monster.

### You will need

stiff card    holepuncher    paper fasteners
thinner card    scissors    coloured sticky paper

Cut out two long thin strips of thick card.
Where will you join them to make the scissors action?

Can you invent a monster eating its prey?

# Design and make a bird which flies

Levers can be used for linkages.
Here is how to make a linkage.

Join three thin pieces of
card with paper fasteners.
Push one and see the others
move.

Or use string and paper
fasteners.
Can you make both levers
move together?

You could use this idea to invent a bird which flaps its
wings.

## You will need

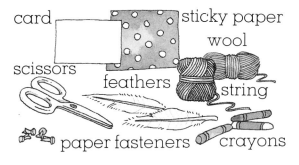

card — sticky paper
wool
scissors
feathers
string
paper fasteners  crayons

Try out a few ideas first.

Linkages can change the
direction of the first force.

# Activity 9

## Send a rocket to the moon

Have you already found out that levers make good rocket launchers?

Here is one to make neatly.

**You will need**

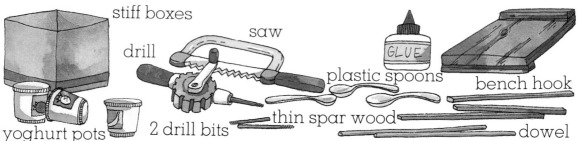

stiff boxes
saw
drill
GLUE
plastic spoons
bench hook
yoghurt pots
2 drill bits
thin spar wood
dowel

Use spar wood for the launcher. Cut it to the size you want. Use dowel for the pivot.

Drill a hole in the launcher for the pivot to go through.

Fix the sides of the pivot to cartons or boxes.

Fix containers to each end of your launcher.

Can you all send a rocket to the moon? Why do some rockets work better than others?

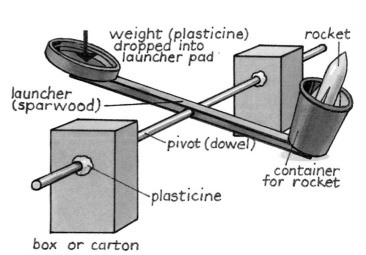

weight (plasticine) dropped into launcher pad
rocket
launcher (sparwood)
pivot (dowel)
container for rocket
plasticine
box or carton

# Roundabouts

Seesaws use machines called levers.
Roundabouts use the wheel, which is also a machine.

You have already found out about wheels in *Wheels on the Bus*.
There are lots more things to find out about wheels.

Have you been on a roundabout at the park or fair?
What did you notice?

Did you notice how you were swung outwards?
Where did this force want to send you?
Where did this force come from?

# Design and make a roundabout

**You will need**

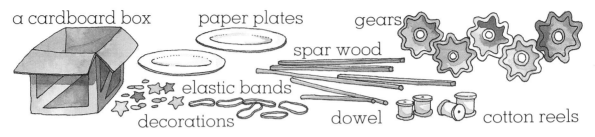

a cardboard box     paper plates     gears     spar wood     elastic bands     decorations     dowel     cotton reels

Have you ideas on how to make a new roundabout? Can you make your roundabout move?

You could make the working parts with gears, or pulleys with cotton reels.

Gears

Cotton reels used as pulleys

Cotton reels stuck together

Work with another person.
Use the Inventor's Roundabout to help you to solve your problems.

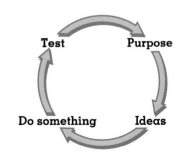

Test     Purpose
Do something     Ideas

# Swings

Do you like the playground swings?
We can find out how they work from looking at the pendulum.

## You will need

paper   string   pen   timer   apple

Tie an apple on to a piece of string and hang it up.

Can you find a way of making it swing for as long as possible without pushing it?
Try out different ideas.
Time how long it took for each of your tests. Make a record.

Afterwards ask yourself:

★ When did it swing the longest? Why?
★ Where did it get its energy from to swing?
★ Why did it stop swinging?

What would happen if you ate half the apple?
Try it out!

## Design and make a swing

A real swing is different to a pendulum. It gains some energy from the people pushing it as well as the force of gravity.

Design and make a swing to put in your playground.

Try and visit a park.
Go on the swings. Find out about the pushing and pulling forces.
Think about the forces the swing must withstand.

**You will need**
your choice of materials from the junk box

Use the Inventor's Roundabout to help you to solve your problems.

# The slide

How does the slide work?

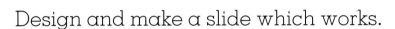

★ When does it work well?
★ When does it work badly?

Design and make a slide which works.

Think carefully about the problem.

Draw some ideas. Try a few out with different materials.
Do some sliding tests with the materials. Keep a record of the tests.

Choose the idea which works best.
Decide on how you will make it. Now make your slide.

**You will need**

card  paper tubes  your own ideas for the sliding part

doll  masking tape  lolly sticks

Does it work?

# Activity 15

## The playground

Make a model playground for all the toys you have made.

Have you an idea for a new toy which no-one has ever thought of?

Make some designs.

Try to think of something different and exciting.

Will children enjoy using it?